Original title:
Citrus Rain

Author: Zachary Prescott

ISBN HARDBACK: 978-1-80586-373-1
ISBN PAPERBACK: 978-1-80586-845-3

Sunlit Nectar from the Clouds

Oh, look! It's coming down, so sweet,
A zesty splash right on your feet.
Dancing droplets, yellow and bright,
Splashing smiles from morning to night.

Lemon mists in the air we breathe,
Careful now, don't slip on the weave!
Grapefruit giggles float into the breeze,
As laughter rolls through the tangy trees.

Sunrise in the Rain

When dawn breaks with a pop and fizz,
The sky's a blender, oh what a whiz!
Orange showers, just a little quirky,
Drenching the world in a zestful smirky.

Sipping puddles like a fancy drink,
Giddy drops make everyone wink.
Morning whispers in a juicy tone,
Bright fruits bouncing, never alone.

Citrus Ripples

Puddles pool with fruity flair,
Jump right in—let’s have a dare!
Bouncing, splashing, it’s quite a show,
Juicy giggles, come join the flow.

Tiny droplets dance on the ground,
It’s a fruity circus, joy unbound.
We’re making rainbows with every step,
Cracking jokes, no room for a prep.

Harvesting Joy from the Ether

In the field where the giggles grow,
The sunbeams tickle, soft and slow.
Fruits fall like laughter from the sky,
Watch out below, it’s a sweet supply!

With baskets brimming and hearts so light,
We catch the giggles flying in flight.
A playful harvest, sunshine's friend,
Squeeze the day, let the laughter blend.

A Drizzle of Golden Cheer

Droplets fall like lemonade,
Puddles form, a sweet charade.
Children splash in citrus pools,
Wearing smiles, nobody mules.

Lemons dance upon the street,
Oranges twirl on happy feet.
Laughter bubbles, joy unfolds,
In this rain, life's fun retold.

Refreshing Scent of the Gale

Whiffs of zest upon the breeze,
Tickling noses, just like tease.
A sudden splash of fruity fun,
As summer storms are on the run.

Umbrellas turned to fruit stands fast,
Giggles roar as the storm blasts.
Nature's jive, a silly game,
Where every drop does dance and claim.

The Twilight Citrus Glow

As dusk descends with twinkling zest,
Grapefruits roll, a funny quest.
They bounce around with all their might,
Chasing shadows into the night.

The moonlight laughs, it too can see,
How silly fruits can dance so free.
A wobbly walk, a twinkling flight,
In twilight's glow, they shine so bright.

Tangy Thunders

The clouds rumble with a giggle loud,
As limes laugh under the gathering cloud.
Tartness drops like chuckles from the sky,
With each burst, the laughter flies high.

Each thunderclap, a citrus cheer,
With every splash, we hold them dear.
A comedy of flavors on the rise,
In this storm, joy and zest surprise.

Tangy Drizzles

When the sky starts to squirt, oh what a sight,
Lemon drops dance, a zesty delight.
Oranges roll by on a squishy parade,
I dodge the swift slices, oh, how they've strayed.

A grapefruit tumble makes my dog bark,
He slips on the peel, aimed for the park.
Squeezed by the chaos, I cannot refrain,
Laughing and dodging this fruity domain.

The Juicy Whisper of Clouds

Bubbles of flavor float down from the blue,
A citrusy giggle in each little dew.
Lemonade rivers flow past my bare toes,
Splashing sweet sunshine wherever it goes.

A slip on a wedge sends me twirling around,
Laughing with lemons, my laughter profound.
For every twist comes a squeezy surprise,
Joy fills the puddles beneath lemony skies.

Sunburst in the Downpour

Spritz from above, it’s a high-flying fling,
Sunshine and tang begin to take wing.
The clouds burst with laughter, a vibrant display,
Citron confetti brightens my day.

Umbrellas turned upside-down in the breeze,
Digesting the joy while inhaling the z's.
I’m caught in a downpour of giggles and zest,
This wacky wet wonder is simply the best!

Limoncello Dreams

In a world where puddles are pockets of cheer,
Gummy bears swim, flavored without fear.
Sip on the skies, stretch your arms wide,
As candies come raining, let laughter be your guide.

A citrusy twist makes the ground dance a jig,
While lollipops bounce, oh so big!
With each splash I skip, my worries outweigh,
In dreams full of sweetness, I'll tango all day.

The Flavor of Falling Water

When droplets tumble from the sky,
They taste like lemons, oh my my!
A sip of sunshine with every splash,
Puddles of punch make quite a bash.

Umbrellas turned to giant plates,
Catch the drips; it’s what awaits!
We dance and twist to citrus tunes,
While sipping zest from silver spoons.

Squeeze of the Storm

A storm approaches with a grin,
Out pops the juicer; let’s begin!
Limes and oranges whirl around,
We’re blending laughs with the wet ground.

Rain coats actors in a play,
Oranges chase the clouds away.
Hilarity's fruit flies through the air,
Pints of juice and citrus flair!

Sweetness in the Clouds

Above us floats a fluffy treat,
With gummy bears and joy to eat.
Lemon lollipops swirl and sway,
As we skip through this fruity day.

Clouds burst open, filled with zest,
A splash of humor is the best.
We giggle as the tangy drops,
Create a puddle of sweets, and hops.

Aroma of Golden Drops

Golden droplets, a citrus spark,
Turn each rainy day to a lark.
Lemonade rivers flow through the night,
With giggles bubbling, oh what a sight!

We sniff the air, it smells so bright,
Squeezy laughter in pure delight.
Friends together beneath the trees,
Tasting joy in a summer breeze.

Nectar from Heaven

Droplets of orange, a sweet little tease,
Dancing on rooftops, like a band of freeze.
Lemon drops giggle, while limes spin around,
In this zesty downpour, joy knows no bound.

Sipping the laughter, with a sour twist,
Puddles of flavor, you simply can't resist.
Rubber duckies float, made of limey zest,
In a splashy parade, life’s colorful quest.

Surreal Citrus Dreams

In a world of limes, oh what a sight!
Chasing grapefruit clouds, in the soft moonlight.
A tangerine sun, with a grin so wide,
Squirrels in raincoats, slipping with pride.

Tartness in the air, like a ticklish breeze,
Bananas in bow ties, dancing with ease.
Frogs wearing hats, sipping fruit punch drinks,
Laughing at sunshine, while the whole world winks.

Zestful Showers

A waterfall of zest, splashing with cheer,
Oranges do a jig, as lemons draw near.
Dancing puddles giggle, in this citrus spree,
While rubbery raindrops sing a melody.

Limes wear little boots, tap-dancing on grass,
Grapefruits twirl round, in a slow-motion pass.
With each lemon drop's bounce, laughter takes flight,
In this sweet serenade, everything feels right.

Squeeze of the Sky

Up above the town, the heavens are bright,
With sweet little bursts of flavor, pure delight.
Honeyed laughter spills, in zesty delight,
As fruits share their secrets, under the moonlight.

Pineapples in parachutes, drifting with glee,
Catching ripe whispers, from the tops of the trees.
With every squishy step, a giggle escapes,
In this charming adventure, everyone shapes.

The Burst Before the Deluge

One orange fell from the sky,
It shouted, "Look, I can fly!"
Lemon drops danced on the ground,
While grapefruits rolled all around.

The neighbor slipped on a peel,
Screamed, "I should've known this deal!"
With laughter echoing in the air,
We all joined in—who needs a chair?

Harvest of Raindrops

We gathered fruit on a bright day,
But juicy clouds had come to play.
A splash here, a splash there, oh my!
It seems our harvest learned to fly.

With goggles on, we took our stand,
As tangerines fell like soft sand.
They bounced around like laughing friends,
With every drip, the fun never ends.

Zesty Puddles

Puddles brightened the gray street,
Each wave gave a tangy treat.
We splashed and slipped in bright delight,
As oranges danced in sheer delight.

The laughter rose, as zests flew high,
A squishy slide, oh my, oh my!
Who needs a water park today?
When juicy drops come out to play!

Aroma of the Tropics

A scent so sweet filled the air,
Tropical breezes, without a care.
The scent of zest turned into glee,
As we all joined for a fruity spree.

Mangoes mixed with lime and cheer,
Creating giggles far and near.
In this fragrant, wacky domain,
We danced beneath the golden rain.

Sun-Soaked Clouds

Fluffy clouds parade so bright,
Dancing round in pure delight.
With every giggle, they release,
A splash of joy, a warm increase.

They whisper secrets, playfully tease,
Tickle your toes, bring you to your knees.
Sunshine's smile, a vibrant thrill,
Makes puddles laugh and windows chill.

The Scent of Unexpected Storms

A whiff of zesty, jolly air,
Rolling thunder, without a care.
Lemon drops begin to sprinkle,
Silly noses start to tinkle.

Raindrops giggle, plop, and sway,
Making puddles join the play.
Unexpected, yet it's clear,
A fruity fiesta is drawing near!

Morning Dew on Citrus Leaves

Morning breaks with playful quirks,
Dewdrops dance like tiny smirks.
On green leaves, they pop and roll,
Riddles of joy that tickle the soul.

They bounce around in sunny glee,
Creating a soundtrack of giddy spree.
Nature's fun, in every drop,
A chorus of laughter—never stop!

Gold Drops from Above

Gold drops tumble from the sky,
Like cheeky sprites, they zoom and fly.
With every splash, a giggle shakes,
As silly smiles ignite what wakes.

They shimmer bright on streets and hair,
Turning frowns to joyous flair.
A golden shower, oh what fun!
Life's a party, and we're all spun!

Sweet Symphony of Nature's Delight

The tree swings low, a fruit's parade,
Lemons rolling, a citrus charade.
The oranges giggle, a zesty cheer,
As squirrels dance round, their cheeks full of beer.

Limes spin tales of sunshine's grin,
While grapefruits plot their juicy win.
In this orchard, laughter takes flight,
As fruits hold court in a fruity delight.

After the Storm: A Tangy Harvest

Rain made the lemons dance with glee,
They wore tiny boots, quite a sight to see.
Grapes rolled in puddles like little round balls,
While the thunder clapped, as the citrus calls.

The storm passed, revealing a fragrant spree,
Fruits held a party, come taste with me!
The clouds laughed too as they drifted away,
Leaving behind a feast for the day.

Glazed with Essence

Zesty donuts fresh from the oven's glow,
Covered in sprinkles, oh how they flow!
A tangerine twist, a lemony spin,
The sugary laughter begins with a grin.

Each bite a burst, a joyful delight,
Like dancing marbles, it’s quite the sight.
Frosted with joy, we all come alive,
In this sweet glaze, good vibes will thrive.

Morning's Juicy Embrace

Morning sunlight on a citrus kiss,
A playful start, how could we miss?
With pancakes stacked, topped high and bright,
Orange syrup drizzles, what a sweet sight!

Coffee winking, with a zesty tease,
As the toast crunches with a joyful ease.
Every bite bursts like confetti in air,
Morning's embrace, so juicy and rare.

Juice Drops from the Sky

When the clouds start to squirt,
You better grab a skirt.
Lemonade rivers flow,
As puddles start to glow.

People dance in the street,
With oranges on their feet.
Sipping from their hats,
Laughing with the chitchats.

Fruit flies join the fun,
Bouncing like they've just run.
Umbrellas turned inside out,
Sour giggles twist about.

So next time you hear a splash,
Get ready for a fruity bash.
Splashing juice on the ground,
Who knew fun could be so round?

Zestful Showers

The weather looks a bit bright,
But citrus is taking flight.
Limes leap from the sky,
With grapefruit's joyful sigh.

Kids with cups in their hands,
Running through wet, gooey lands.
Slipping, sliding in cheer,
Zesty giggles, oh so near!

Mom's pie on the rooftop,
Sours landed with a plop.
Neighbors peek through their blinds,
Wondering what this finds.

So grab your ball and your towel,
Join the juicy, happy howl.
When it rains fruit instead,
Who cares what the forecast said?

Sunlit Drizzle

Golden drops start to shine,
Drizzling tangy grape and brine.
Collecting in every nook,
Like a juicy fairy book.

Dogs chase after the light,
Puppies pounced in pure delight.
Tails wagging like a breeze,
Running past the lemon trees.

Picnics now take a twist,
Sandwiches in the mist.
Sunlight dancing in the air,
Tasting joy without a care.

When the sun begins to gleam,
Chasing clouds is quite the dream.
With a splash and a squeal,
The fun’s as real as a meal!

Tangy Drenched Dreams

In a land where fruits can float,
And limes can barely gloat,
The world is flipped upside down,
With every juicy little frown.

Dancing under a tangerine,
What a colorful, wacky scene.
Sipping juice from a shoe,
Watch out, it might squirt you too!

Sock puppets made of zest,
Hold a talent show, no rest.
With laughs thick enough to spread,
And dreams tossed where they're fed.

So if you're feeling quite blue,
Let the juice drip down on you.
Life's a party made of fun,
When the sweetest drops have run!

Lemon Drops on Leaves

Tiny drops that bounce and play,
They giggle in the sun all day.
Each one rolls with a silly grin,
A zesty dance where fun begins.

A twisty path of twirling zest,
They ponder which drop is the best.
With every bounce, they're sure to spill,
A sunny punch of juice and thrill.

When clouds arrive, they all conspire,
To create a splash, they never tire.
But watch your step, for slippery fun,
Can land you in a squeeze, oh what a run!

With laughter loud, the leaves rejoice,
In every drop, you hear a voice.
They sing of joy, they sing of cheer,
In nature's party, we all appear.

Orange Mist at Dawn

A misty veil in the morning light,
Orange dreams take off in flight.
They tickle noses, quench the air,
With giggles of joy everywhere.

Like spray from a jolly fruit machine,
They swirl and dance, a joyous scene.
Bouncing rays and citrus cheer,
The dawn brings laughter, loud and clear.

Puppies chase the orange breeze,
As sunlit giggles rustle trees.
They tumble through the sizzling grass,
In this zesty morn, let time just pass.

A tickly mist, a warm embrace,
Nature's game of hide and chase.
Each breath a giggle, bright and bold,
In the orange glow, just watch it unfold.

The Aroma of Sunlit Storms

When thunder rumbles, the fun begins,
A twist of fragrance, spice and wins.
The air's alive with playful scents,
As sunshine mingles with the suspense.

Sour notes and sweet collide,
Creating laughter, pure and wide.
Raindrops tiptoe, a splashing tease,
Sprinkling gold on all the trees.

Then comes the giggle of lightning's flash,
With rumbling giggles that make a splash.
A tap-dance beat on rooftops play,
In scented storms, we sway away.

The world spins wild in citrus charm,
While stormy laughter brings no harm.
Every storm, a playful game,
With aromas dancing, who needs fame?

Grapefruit Serenade

In gardens lush with bouncy blooms,
A grapefruit sings in sunny rooms.
With every note, a joyful twist,
It serenades, you cannot miss.

Its laughter echoes, bright and round,
In every chord, sweet joy is found.
Each juicy verse, a zany rhyme,
Making moments feel sublime.

Tickling noses with fragrant flair,
It tosses giggles in the air.
A zesty sonnet, fresh and bold,
Tales of bliss and fun retold.

So come and sway in this delight,
Dance with the fruit, it feels so right.
Grapefruit laughs as evening falls,
In cheerful tunes, the world enthralls.

Orange Rainscape

When droplets start to jive,
In a zesty, wobbly dive,
Lemons laugh, and limes all sing,
As fruit flies take to wing.

A dribble and a splash, oh dear,
Peeling oranges brings good cheer,
We'll dance beneath the yellow sky,
With giggles as the puddles dry.

Let's juggle all the citrus snacks,
While avoiding juice-filled tracks,
Each burst bursts forth a sunny grin,
As laughter tickles from within.

So grab your boots and don't be late,
To skip through fruit and contemplate,
That every squirt from fruit so bright,
Is simply nature's funny sight!

Tang of Earth in the Air

The air is flavored, can’t you see?
A fruity scent that tickles me,
With every step, the ground does squish,
Like landing on a citrus wish.

A pickle dance with orange zest,
What a day, we’ve been quite blessed,
If lemons fall, we’ll catch the fun,
In puddles bright, we’ll splash and run.

The clouds parade a juicy tease,
As grapefruits roll upon the breeze,
Sticky fingers, sweetened cheeks,
And hearty laughs, that’s what life seeks.

Oh, the tangy breeze that we adore,
Makes grumpy frowns hit the floor,
With citrus whims and giggly airs,
We’ll skip through life without any cares!

Fragrant Morsels from the Sky

When skies decide to throw a feast,
I grab a bucket, to say the least,
With every splash, a smelly treat,
A dance of juice beneath our feet.

The grapefruits chuckle, oranges cheer,
As rainbows bend, we shed a tear,
Of laughter shared in fruity glee,
A goofy night of zest, you see!

I caught a slice that flew right past,
With citrus smiles that dance so fast,
On sticky toes, we spin and twirl,
As fruity morsels softly swirl.

When dinner calls, let's skip the cake,
For juicy drops, oh what a break,
We'll savor sunbeams, rain's delight,
And feast on joy, from day to night!

A Splash of Sunkissed Bliss

In a world where rainbows bloom,
Like fruit trees dancing in full room,
With every splash in sunny haze,
We celebrate the zesty craze.

Lemon drops from great heights fall,
Twisting, swirling—what a ball!
We'll juggle limes like they're our kin,
And bubble up with giggles within.

A splash of joy as oranges glide,
Through raucous laughter, side by side,
We wrestle with these juicy beams,
As fun drips like our silly dreams.

So come and sip the golden tease,
Where laughter drips like honeyed breeze,
With every squirt, the world's in bliss,
Each drop a fruity, cheeky kiss!

Liquid Sunshine

Drip, drop, a zesty sound,
Puddles forming on the ground.
With a squirt, I take a sip,
Watch my friends do a slip!

Bouncing lemons in a dance,
Caught in a cheery trance.
Lime green shoes upon my feet,
Skipping to this bright beat.

Squeeze of joy in every rain,
Why not dance away the pain?
Grapefruit hats and orange coats,
Wobbling like silly goats!

A splash here, a splash there,
Who knew fruit could fill the air?
With each giggle, joy does swell,
From the drizzle, we all fell!

Citrus Burst in the Breeze

Whirling, twirling, citrus flight,
Grapes join in, what a sight!
Lemonade clouds float above,
Chasing giggles, full of love.

In the kitchen, spoons do gleam,
Mixing magic, what a dream!
Juicy droplets, cheeky smiles,
Rolling laughter, miles and miles.

Mangoed mists and orange skies,
Silly birds in fruit disguise.
With each squirt, a chuckle flies,
As the sun begins to rise.

Swirls of zest in every breath,
Bursting laughter, life from death.
With a wink and lemon twist,
It's a party you can't resist!

Fragrant Drops on Petal Paths

Petals dance in purple hue,
Fragrant drops that taste like dew.
Bees are buzzing, what a show,
Chasing scents where giggles grow.

Wading through the sugary mist,
Accidental fruit-filled twist.
Squeezed my way into the fun,
Now I'm bright like morning sun.

Ripe with laughter, hear the sound,
Bouncing glories all around.
Footprints muddied, sweet and bright,
Slipping laughter through the night.

Grapefruits giggle, lemons sing,
This delight's a crazy thing.
Running wild, a fruity chime,
Such delight, we've lost all time!

Light's Juicy Tears

Drip, drop, a silly slosh,
Watch me dance and take a nosh.
Light in droplets, laughing clear,
Wipe my face, it's sweet, I swear!

With each sprinkle, don’t you grin?
A citrus shower, let’s begin!
Splat of joy, it hits my nose,
What a game, who really knows?

Bouncing raspberries overhead,
Wacky fruit makes us turn red.
Tangerine twirls in the air,
Laughing fruit everywhere!

Lemon drops and orange winks,
Sipping life, how the mind blinks.
With each splash, our spirits rise,
Underneath these fruity skies!

Verdant Melodies in the Rain

Droplets bouncing, oh what cheer,
A party in each splash, so clear.
Lemons giggle, oranges dance,
While limes just roll, in a trance.

Funny faces on the ground,
With every plop, new friends are found.
Umbrellas twirl like wild balloons,
As laughter swells with playful tunes.

Trees wear hats of bright yellow hues,
While puddles form, like wiggly pools.
Squirrels slide down the slippery bark,
Creating chaos, igniting a spark.

In this jolly, zesty spree,
Nature's rhythm, wild and free.
So grab a cup, let’s toast in cheer,
To silly storms, their jokes sincere.

Serendipity in Citrus Showers

Umbrellas sprout like mushrooms bright,
While fruits fall down, a zesty sight.
Grapefruits giggle as they slide,
Chasing ducks on a citrus ride.

Pineapples wink, while lemons snore,
Mandarins dancing on the floor.
A slippery path turns into a race,
With every splash, we can't trace.

So here we stomp in puddles wide,
With fruity friends right by our side.
Lemons squirt, a cheeky spray,
We'll laugh and run for another play.

What a ride in these twists and turns,
Through fruity chaos, our spirit burns.
As laughter echoes, let’s boldly declare,
Life's sweeter when we splash without care.

Twilight with a Twist

Night falls down with a zippy zest,
Twisted fruits put laughter to the test.
Juggling lemons under a starry show,
While peppy oranges steal the glow.

Puddles giggle, mocking us so,
With every jump, we hit a new flow.
A comet of limes zooms overhead,
As we dance on the fruit-laden bed.

Bananas slip with the nimblest grace,
While grapefruits roll, not a trace of space.
Twilight chuckles at our scrambles,
As we chase the fruit, with muffled rambles.

So here we stand, in a fruity delight,
With jokes that twinkle in the night.
For in every splash, a chuckle resides,
In this zesty time, our joy collides.

Dewy Grove Serenade

Oh, the grove, it sings with glee,
With citrus smiles all around me.
Lemon trees sway with cheerful tunes,
Beneath the laughs of chubby raccoons.

Frogs in hats croak silly rhymes,
As oranges dance lost in their primes.
A tangerine slips and takes a bow,
While all the critters cheer aloud.

Twinkling stars drop tangy scents,
Where every leaf, in mirth, repents.
Bursts of giggles like sparks in the air,
Funny faces, no worries to bear.

So join the fun in this juicy spree,
As fruits unite in jubilee.
In every droplet, a story to share,
In this dewy grove, love is everywhere.

Refreshing Deluge

When life gives you droplets, wear a hat,
Just watch for the splashes, and avoid the splat.
Lemon drops falling, like candy from the sky,
Grab a cup quickly, shout a fruity 'hi!'

Umbrellas are shields against zesty sweeps,
Jumping in puddles, as laughter creeps.
Oranges are wobbling, rolling down the lane,
Chasing those spheres, oh what a gain!

Sweet little droplets dance on my nose,
Each drop a giggle, unexpected to pose.
Let's taste the laughter, let's savor the fun,
In this wild weather, we're never done!

Squeezed lemons on winds, oh what a blow,
Fruits falling fast, in a colorful show.
Party in the downpour, it's a bold affair,
So come take a dive in this zesty scare!

Citrus Symphony

Melodies bursting, a tangerine tune,
Fruits in the air, are they coming too soon?
Limes are all jiving with a twist and a flip,
Join in the chorus, let's all take a dip!

Grapefruits are giggling, they roll with delight,
Raining down flavors, oh what a sight.
Bananas are dancing, they've lost their composure,
In this funny weather, we embrace the exposure!

Lemons in the key of sunny and bright,
A fruity auction, with none out of sight.
Pineapples plucked from a cloud overhead,
Singing out loud as they tumble and spread!

What's better than laughter when colors collide?
Join this parade as we giggle and glide.
In this zany world where the citrus plays,
Let's splash in the puddles of fruity ballets!

Soft Gush of Tangerine

Hiding from chaos, a tangerine stream,
Spilling and fun, it’s a quirky dream.
Citrus clouds hovering, what will they do?
Orange rain splashes, a riot of hue!

Puddles of flavor, let’s jump in with glee,
Who knew sweet fruits would be falling on me?
Silly old lemons all doing a jig,
Swirling and spinning, oh let’s dance big!

Chasing the zesty, we run and we roar,
Glowing like sunshine, we all want more.
With each gentle shower, a giggle does bounce,
A feast of delights, let’s eat by the ounce!

Every drop’s tickling, so whimsical yet,
In this wacky weather, we’ll never forget.
Soft gushing laughter, on this tangerine spree,
Come join the parade, and just be fruity free!

Raining Fruity Hues

Colors a-dazzle, as drops come alive,
Splashing our spirits, can we ever survive?
Strawberries tumble, like dancers so sweet,
A rainbow of laughter, a vibrant treat!

Pineapples twirling, oh what a sight,
Giggling like children, they dance in the light.
Corny old oranges, they laugh and they play,
In this fruity storm, we'll dance the day away!

Blushing red cherries, on a skip they glide,
Moves are contagious, there's nothing to hide.
Raspberry puddles, a delightful bizarre,
Jumping in joy, we'll be stars from afar!

Why walk when we can hop, skip, and sing?
In this raucous shower, let's savor the fling.
Let's gather the colors, each laugh a bright hue,
In the downpour of fun, it's a fruity review!

The Dance of Acidic Petals

In a garden of zesty glee,
Flowers twirl with a pucker spree.
Bees buzz with a tarty song,
While the lemons dance all day long.

Orange peels take a spin,
Limes join in, with a cheeky grin.
Petals slip, they trip, they slide,
In this fruity, silly ride!

A grapefruit winks from a vine,
Singing sweet like soda's shine.
Their laughter spills like juice out wide,
In their juicy party, they confide.

With every bounce and every jig,
They toss and flip, they dance a dig.
In this fiesta, bright and bold,
A world of giggles, joy untold!

The Lightness of Fruity Breezes

Whispers of tang float through the air,
A playful spark, a fruity flair.
Breeze tickles leaves with a citrus tease,
While clouds giggle, shaking at ease.

Lemon slices grinning wide,
Playful gusts on a merry ride.
Air filled with joy, not a care,
Twirling, swirling, without a spare.

Pineapple clouds drift and sway,
Bouncing high like children at play.
Mango melodies softly chime,
In this lightness, laughter's prime.

Each gust a chuckle, each swirl a grin,
The world spins faster, let the fun begin!
With every breeze, a giggle's-born,
In this air, we are reborn!

Aroma Lingers after the Storm

After the storm, a scent appears,
Zesty laughter clears the tears.
Lingering notes of happy bliss,
Aromatic hugs in a fragrant mist.

Fragrant puddles form a dance,
Where children splash, and lemons prance.
Every droplet sparkles bright,
Under the sun's returning light.

Tangerine twirls in the puddles so,
Creating giggles in water's flow.
Citrus whispers fill the air,
Join the fun without a care.

In the wake of a stormy spree,
Joyful scents, a dancing spree.
With every sniff, we feel alive,
In this zesty world, we thrive!

Sweetness in Every Drop

Out comes the sun, the sweetness flows,
Each drop a laugh, as the citrus glows.
Rainbows burst with a fruity cheer,
As oranges chuckle, 'We're all here!'

Splashing puddles of lemony delight,
Squeezed giggles in the morning light.
Sweetness drips from every tree,
Sticky fingers, pure ecstasy.

Grapefruits bounce like rubber balls,
Every squeeze brings giggles and calls.
In this wonderland, we play,
Chasing moments through the day!

With every sip, a hearty laugh,
Sour is sweet, let's share the path.
Celebrate the drops that fall,
In this juicy world, there's fun for all!

Drops of Joyful Tartness

A zesty splash, oh what a treat,
Lemon drops dance on my feet.
Pineapple giggles, orange sings,
Together they bring such silly things.

Tangerines toss, like peers at play,
Rolling around on a sunny day.
Sour smiles bounce, they don't complain,
In this sweet chaos, we lose our pain.

Limes in hats, with cheeky grins,
They mock each other, yet still are friends.
A fruit parade on rainbow streams,
We laugh along with our juicy dreams.

So grab your cup, let's have a toast,
To the silly fruits we love the most.
In drops of joy, we find our way,
Dancing in sweetness, come what may.

A Symphony of Sunshine and Rain

A fruity orchestra, what a sight,
Melody made of sheer delight.
Strumming grooves of sweet and sour,
In a leafy theater, we all devour.

Grapefruits giggle, the lemons yell,
While orange flutes play a citrus swell.
Beneath the sun, the maracas shake,
Each zephyr brings a fruity quake.

The rain's a turtle, slow and wise,
Wearing raindrops like little pies.
Tropical tunes on a wild balloon,
We bounce to the beat of a fruit-filled tune.

So twist your hips, let laughter ring,
In this jazzy world, the fruits all sing.
Their symphony of sunshine brings,
A giggling night on colorful wings.

Strings of Tangy Light

On a watch that ticks with zest,
Strings of joy, a playful quest.
Limes pluck notes from rainbow skies,
As cherubic cherries wink their eyes.

With plucky tunes and twangy flair,
These lively fruits float in the air.
Each plop and drop releases a giggle,
While we bumble about and wiggle.

Mangoes swing in a bright ballet,
Their sticky sweetness steals the day.
Bananas slip, a cheeky tease,
As grapefruits squeeze with such great ease.

So come one, come all, to this grand show,
Where tangerines dance to and fro.
In strings of light, we'll find our fun,
Join the party until we're done.

The Citrus Caress of Nature

Nature's tickle, vivid and bright,
With zesty whispers that feel just right.
A gentle poke from each sweet fruit,
Makes us laugh and dance in pursuit.

The branches sway, a playful tease,
While fruit balls bounce with a cheeky breeze.
A splash of zest, a hint of cheer,
In nature's arms, we conquer fear.

Tartness tickles, a giddy sneeze,
As we prance 'round the dancing trees.
Every sip is a happy escape,
With vibrant flavors, we all reshape.

So roll in the grass, let laughter reign,
In the tender touch of this sweet domain.
The caress of life, oh what a sight,
Beneath the sun, we revel in light.

The Dewy Citrus Caress

A lemon dropped from high above,
A splash of zest, akin to love.
Orange peels rolled down the street,
Kids slip and slide, leap to their feet.

Grapefruits giggle in the breeze,
Testing fate with such great ease.
A tangerine threw a mighty brawl,
But a lime just laughed, didn't care at all.

In this carnival of tangy thrills,
Where laughter dances, and joy fulfills.
We dodge and dive through citrus cheer,
No need for umbrellas, my friends, oh dear!

So grab your fruit, take a chance,
Join the jolly citrus dance.
With every drop, a burst of glee,
Showered in laughter, wild and free.

Splash of Flavor

A splash of color on my nose,
Lemon slices in rows and rows.
A fruit fight starts, the stakes are high,
Who knew an orange could fly?

Tangerines chuckled from the trees,
As everyone ran with giggles and wheezes.
A creamy pie, oh what a sight,
Accidentally met a grapefruit's bite.

The zest was fierce, the laughter strong,
In the whirlwind of juice where we belong.
Painted faces, a sticky affair,
A tangy wonderland beyond compare.

When life gives flavor, do not frown,
Join the splash party in town!
With every toss and every cheer,
We'll stick together, no need for fear.

Tales from the Zesty Abyss

In a world where lemons reign,
And limes dissolve all stress and strain.
An orange knight with a zestful grin,
Battles citrus foes, let the fun begin!

With every squirt, a story told,
Of crispy peels and treasures bold.
Grapefruits sing, their chorus bright,
While mangoes waltz, what a sight!

Surprises burst from every rind,
In this land where cheer you'll find.
Pick a slice, let laughter roll,
Under the zesty sun, feel whole.

So come partake in fruit-filled glee,
Join the revelry, just you and me!
In the abyss of tang, we rise and fall,
No better place than this fruity hall.

The Lush Downpour

It rained bright wedges in the park,
Juggling slices that left a mark.
A fruit parade, a chance to play,
In the drizzle of zest, we sway!

Bananas slip while grapefruits glide,
Citrus creatures roll and ride.
Pineapples laugh as they tumble down,
Creating a fruity, joyful crown.

We splash and dive in a sea of sweet,
Tasting the laughter with every treat.
Our mugs runneth over with fruity fun,
In this lush downpour, we are one!

So grab your buddies and join the race,
In this fruity flood, we find our place.
With every giggle, we dance with flair,
Embracing the joy of the zestful air.

The Shift of Flavorful Weather

One day the clouds made a zesty show,
With lemons dancing to a raucous flow.
Oranges giggled as they spun around,
Splashing everyone with their merry sound.

The sun yelled, 'Hey! This is quite absurd!'
As grapefruit burst forth, not a single word.
Lime squirts flying like little darts,
Made the day laugh with its juicy arts.

Rhythms of the Fruity Sky

Bananas swayed with a twirl and twist,
While cherries chuckled, they couldn't resist.
The whole sky jived with a fruity beat,
Beneath it, folks shuffled their dancing feet.

"Let's squeeze this fun!" proclaimed a bright peach,
"Be careful, or else it might slip and breach!"
With a slapstick skit in this playful scene,
The fruity showdown was truly serene.

Pomegranate Whispers in the Rain

Pomegranates laughed at the droplets' flow,
"As juicy pearls fall, let's put on a show!"
They sprinkled sparkle on everyone near,
Making cheeks rosy and laughter appear.

The tartness giggled behind a big cloud,
"Come join our party, it's noisy and loud!"
Juggling zest and sweet, they surely shined,
Creating a ruckus, with smiles combined.

The Cloud's Citrus Lullaby

In the sky high above, a sweet chorus played,
With tangerines humming, not one bit afraid.
While plump limes floated on fluffy white fluff,
The whole world giggled, this feeling was tough.

Lemons rolled down like soft little balls,
Bouncing and bouncing, ignoring the falls.
The world swirled 'round in a colorful spree,
Under this blanket of fruity glee.

A Symphony of Citrus Clouds

In the sky, a twist of zest,
Lemons dance, they look their best.
Clouds giggle in a tangy spree,
Sipping sun; oh, come with me!

Oranges chuckle, 'Let's have fun!'
While tangerines bask in the sun.
Raindrops burst with flavors bright,
A fruity party, pure delight!

Grapefruits roll, a playful set,
Chasing blooms; it's quite a bet.
Lime slices spin in whirlpool glee,
Dancing wildly, oh look at me!

The air's so sweet, it tickles pink,
With every drop, our spirits link.
So grab a glass, don't sit and dwell,
In this zesty vesel, all is well!

Refreshing Mist on Grove Green

A splash of juice, a burst of cheer,
Lemonade whispers, 'Come near, my dear!'
In the grove, where giggles grow,
A sprinkle of joy, just let it flow!

Limes giggle, their hats askew,
While trying to dance, quite out of view.
Grapefruit jokes, so sour and sweet,
Squeeze out the laughter, feel the beat!

Amidst the trees, we spin and twirl,
With every splash, we leap and whirl.
The grass is sticky, the fun's not done,
A fruity romp, we laugh and run!

So here we stand, with juice in hand,
In the lively grove, life’s unplanned.
With scents so bright, let’s dance and sing,
In this fragrant mist, joy's the king!

Limoncello Skies

Under skies of lemon glow,
Sunshine spritzes a lovely show.
A toast to laughter, tangy delight,
Joy bubbles up, oh what a sight!

Pineapple plays hopscotch along,
Zesty tunes where we belong.
With every splash, a chuckle loud,
Celebrating life, we're citrus proud!

Marshmallow clouds, so soft and bright,
Catch their puddles; it's pure delight!
Jokes squeezed tight, like peels on fruit,
With every giggle, our friendship's root!

So dance away in this vibrant haze,
Under limoncello's glistening rays.
Life's a jest, a sip from the bowl,
With every splash, we find our role!

The Taste of Thunder

With splashes bold, the skies collide,
Oranges roll, they cannot hide.
A zesty laugh as raindrops sing,
There's something fun in this crazy fling!

A tangy burst, a twist of fate,
Grapefruits juggle, oh what a state!
With every boom, the laughter grows,
Sour and sweet in weather blows!

So let it pour, let spirits ride,
With lemonade rivers, let's enjoy the tide.
In fruity storms, we laugh and cheer,
Each taste of thunder, we hold dear!

Join the party, don't miss a beat,
With every sprinkle, let's move our feet.
In this zany sky, fun's the key,
Come taste the thunder; it's wild and free!

A Serenade for Tart Souls

In a grove where the lemons might sing,
The sour notes make the jester's heart cling.
A dance with the limes, oh what a feat,
With splashes of flavor, bitterness sweet.

If oranges giggle and grapefruits pout,
The zest in the air makes laughter sprout.
Slip on a peel, take a tumble, then cheer,
For a citrusy jest is always near.

A drop on the cheek, oh what a delight,
As flavors explode in a tart little bite.
Juggling fruit like a clown at the fair,
Tart souls find solace in zest everywhere.

So come join the party, the fruit's in a spin,
With every sour giggle, let the fun begin.
A serenade sung in a tangy parade,
For the silly, the fruity, a joyful charade.

Essence of Sunshine in Each Drop

A splash of yellow, a squeeze so bright,
Each drop tells a tale of pure delight.
Lemonade rivers where laughter cascades,
Chasing the blues with each sip that invades.

A glass half-full means joy's overflowing,
With every sip, the giggles keep growing.
Sunny droplets dance, primed for a laugh,
Wear your fruit hat, and let's do the math!

Oranges wink as they roll down the stream,
Citrusy wishes and a dairy queen dream.
Pour on the sunshine, let spirits lift high,
With essence so bright, you'll soar to the sky.

Join us in laughter, as tangy drops flow,
The essence of fun, like a playful glow.
So raise up your glasses, the jokes never stop,
With sunshine in droplets, we're ready to hop.

Amber Thunder

In the storm of flavor, a thunder rolls,
With hints of sweetness that tickle our souls.
Amber drops fall, like playful little bombs,
Exploding with giggles in citrusy qualms.

The clouds burst open, a zesty encore,
Singing rainbows of laughter, we can’t ignore.
Squeeze in some fun as we dance in the wet,
Bathing in sunshine, we laugh and we fret.

Each droplet's a jester, a wild caricature,
Swirling in chaos, but never unsure.
Amber thunder shakes up the tedium tight,
Let’s roll in the rain and find joy in the night.

So come be the sunshine amid the loud roar,
With citrusy giggles that we can't ignore.
As the amber clouds paint a zany new scene,
In a world full of laughter, our spirits are keen.

Rhapsody in Zest

Let’s toast to the tang, the zest of our days,
With citrusy choruses in cheerful arrays.
A rhapsody sung with a hint of a laugh,
Each note a reminder, let’s rewrite the path.

From lemons to limes, let the melodies flow,
With grooves that shake up even the slow.
Twist in the rhythm, let’s stir up the fun,
As zesty adventures have only begun.

Grapefruits are grooving, they’re leading the band,
While oranges roll in with a tangerine hand.
A jam session sparkles, oh what a delight,
With fruity compositions that dance through the night.

So gather around, be it day or be night,
With rhapsodies zesty, our hearts feel so light.
In this citrusy concert, there’s laughter and cheer,
As every bright note pulls the world ever near.

Lemonade Skies

The clouds are squeezed like lemons,
With flavors that bounce and play.
Sunshine giggles with a twist,
As laughter pours in bright array.

Jugs of joy spill all around,
While sprightly drops make rooftops gleam.
Rainbows dance in glassy fair,
As we all sip from the stream.

Slippery sidewalks, a zesty slip,
A lemonade splash, a sudden cheer.
We spin and twirl in sweet delight,
While friends and citrus dance near.

So raise a glass to the oddball skies,
Where joy and tang are quite the sight.
With every drop a giggle flows,
And life tastes good, bubbly and bright.

Fruitful Tear of Heaven

The heavens shed a playful mix,
With little round drops full of fun.
Each splash brings giggles to our lips,
As we run, skip, and dash in the sun.

A wobbly orange rolls on by,
Chasing a lemon in a race.
Puddles bubble with fruity zest,
As we jump in without a trace.

With clouds that pop like fizzy drinks,
We dance through this zany delight.
It's a wild fruit party outside,
Where every tear feels just right.

So let the world giggle with us,
As we splash through this lively scene.
For in this chaos of cheerful drops,
Life’s sweetest moments can be seen.

Bright Drops of Zestful Light

Pitter-patter, what a sight,
Zesty smiles in the air.
Lemon drops from shelves of blue,
Encouraging a chuckle to share.

With every splash, we take a turn,
Banana peels make us slide.
Sticky fingers, juicy joy,
With laughter flooding wide-eyed.

Puddle jumping, citrus-filled,
A parade of funny tunes.
As fruits unite within the clouds,
Dance of brightness, no more glooms.

So let's embrace this bright affair,
With zesty winds upon our face.
Here’s to drops that make us grin,
In a world of fun-filled space.

Sweet Storm of Citrus

A storm brews with a giggly swirl,
As oranges fall like jolly beads.
Tangerines bounce on sidewalks slick,
While laughter is the rain that leads.

We open up our mouths with glee,
Ready for a fruity shower.
Sour surprises come our way,
But joy adds to the lasting power.

Limes and lemons skip and hop,
With punchy splashes that amuse.
In each puddle, a joke is found,
As laughter brightens all our views.

So here's to storms that bring delight,
With tangy bursts of joy in tow.
We dance beneath a fruity storm,
As the world around us starts to glow.

Drizzle of Delight

A sprinkle of sunshine, a splash of zest,
Lemons in puddles, the tangiest jest.
Oranges are laughing, in the clouds they play,
As limes dance with joy, on a bright sunny day.

With each little drop, a giggle escapes,
As fruits wear their hats, and dance with grapes.
The sky throws a party, in yellow and green,
Silly fruit shindig, quite the funny scene.

A tangerine trumpet sounds loud and clear,
As cherries join in, bringing plenty of cheer.
In a whirl of flavors, the laughter takes flight,
Who knew rain could bring such delight?

The raindrops keep splashing, oh what a sight,
With every little bounce, they're feeling just right.
So we twirl in the drizzle, a fruity parade,
Laughing at nature's sweet escapade.

Brightness Between the Storms

When clouds start to grumble, and thunder roars near,
A burst of bright colors will always appear.
A wink from a lemon, a jig from a pear,
In the dance of the raindrops, we all have to share.

Pineapples giggle in droplets of fun,
While mangoes on lemonade take off and run.
The fruit salad crew can't help but rejoice,
In the midst of the tempest, they make a loud noise.

A twist of bright laughter, a splash from above,
With every sweet drizzle, they feel all the love.
Raindrops like candy, so tasty and round,
Between all the storms, happiness is found.

So let's raise a glass to this fruity delight,
For even in showers, the future looks bright.
With smiles and with giggles, let's weather it right,
In the brightness of laughter, we take to flight.

Citrus Reverie

Dancing in puddles, the grapefruits unite,
With zesty little giggles, oh what a sight!
Their dreams made of juice, they swirl and they spin,
As the world drinks their laughter from deep within.

Under the clouds, they share their sweet tales,
Of slapstick adventures, and fruity details.
The oranges all snicker as they start to roll,
In a whirl of delight, they capture the soul.

With laughter so bright, it can soften the gray,
Like jellybean dreams that have come out to play.
The lemons are winking, the limes keep the beat,
With every ridiculous move, they feel so sweet.

In this reverie, they pop and they fizz,
As the funny fruit festival buzzes and whizzes.
Let's twirl through the laughter, let's splash in the zest,
In this world full of smiles, we all are the best.

Summer's Sweet Sprinkles

Oh, summer's a sprinkle of juice and good cheer,
With fruity confetti that dances all near.
A burst of bright laughter, like stars in the sky,
With each little drizzle, we giggle and fly.

Limes throw a splash, just to catch our surprise,
And lemons will wink with their bright-beaming eyes.
Citrus confessions from oranges sway,
As tropical breezes come out to play.

Pineapples crack jokes and mangoes just grin,
All fruits are invited to join the sweet spin.
With each little drop that comes down like a treat,
The summer feels silly, the laughter's elite.

So let's soak in the sprinkles, enjoy the zest,
In this funny fruit party, we're truly blessed.
With every good giggle, we brighten the day,
In the sweetness of summer, we dance and we sway.

www.ingramcontent.com/pod-product-compliance
Lightning Source LLC
Chambersburg PA
CBHW070316120526
44590CB00017B/2706
* 9 7 8 1 8 0 5 8 6 8 4 5 3 *